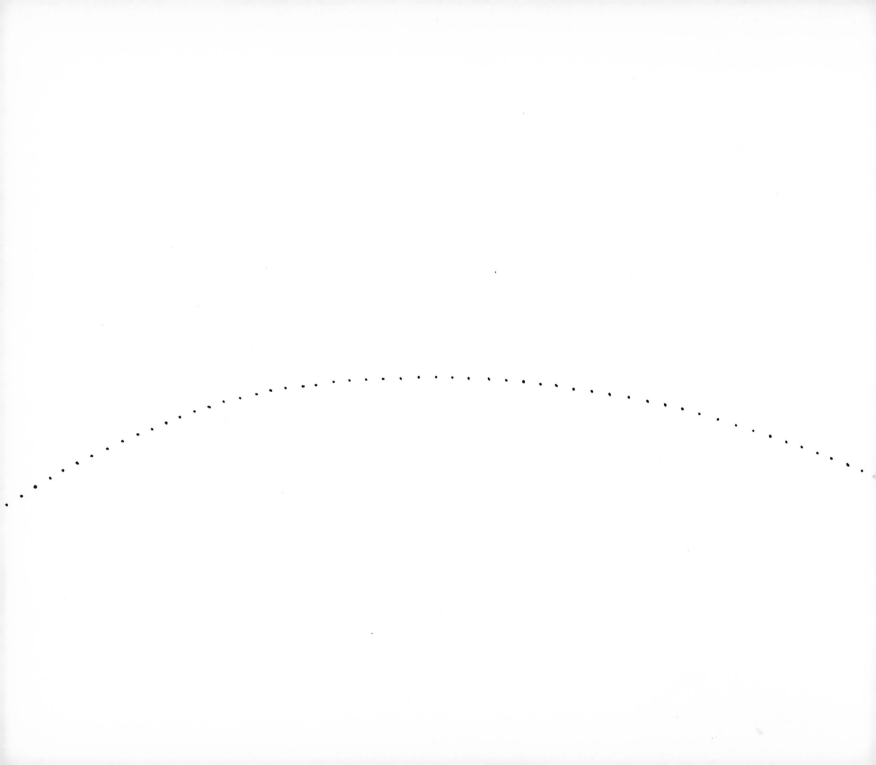

WHAT COLOR AM I?

Written by LOYAL NYE • Illustrated by RICK DAVIS

ABINGDON • NASHVILLE

WHAT COLOR AM I?

ISBN 0-687-44633-3

Library of Congress Cataloging in Publication Data

NYE, LOYAL.
What color am I?

SUMMARY: Explores the various manifestations of color in
our world especially the different shades of people skins.
1. Race awareness—Juvenile literature. [1. Race awareness. 2. Color of man. 3. Christian life] I. Davis, Rick. II. Title.
BF724.3.R3N9   301.45' 1' 042   76-55577

For: the children of the Christian Day School of Warner Memorial Presbyterian Church and particularly Shannon Kelly

To open a child's eyes is a special gift. It is hoped that this book will do just that. For this reason the illustrations were planned to convey a sense of color and shape rather than detail. Because God created and continues to re-create the world according to His plan, both past and present tenses are used.

When God planned the world,
He must have loved color very much.
He chose a beautiful blue for the sky
and green for the grass and trees.

He planned pure white
for clouds.
    Then
the yellow sun changes them
to pink and silver and violet.

When God planned flowers,
He didn't want them all
to be just alike.

To make the world
more interesting,
He made the flowers
different colors
and different shapes.

When God planned people
He didn't want them all
to be alike either.

Some are **tall** and some are short.

Some are **fat** and some are thin.

Some are **big** and some are small.

To make the world still more interesting,
God chose colors for His people, too.
But these were different colors
from the ones He chose for flowers
and the rest of the world.

We say some people are white,
but God really didn't
                    make
                        people
                            white.

Put your hand on this page. This page is white. Is your hand white?

No.

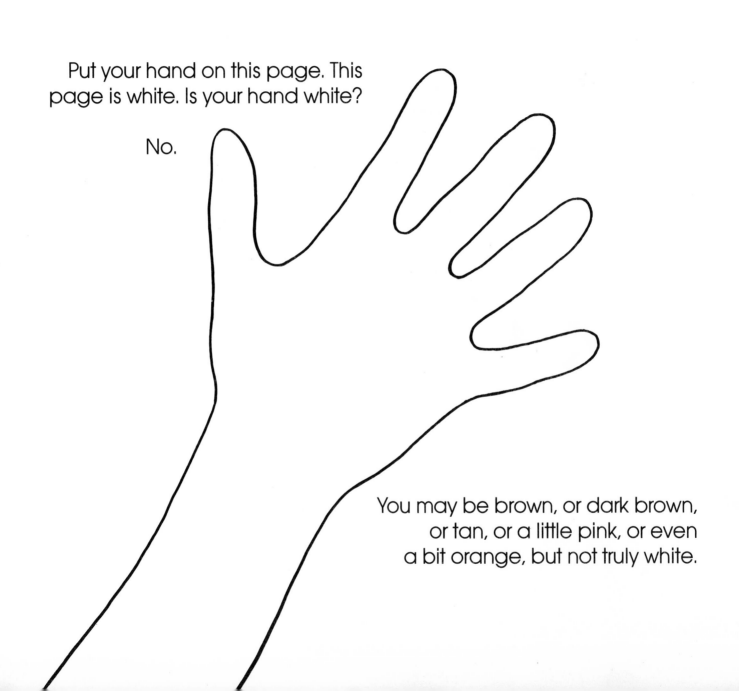

You may be brown, or dark brown, or tan, or a little pink, or even a bit orange, but not truly white.

God
saved white for clouds
and snow

and Easter lilies and daisies.

Could your hand be yellow?

No.

Sometimes we say there are yellow people.
But there aren't really yellow people.
God saved pure yellow
for lemons

and sunflowers

and daffodils.

Could your hand
be red?

No.

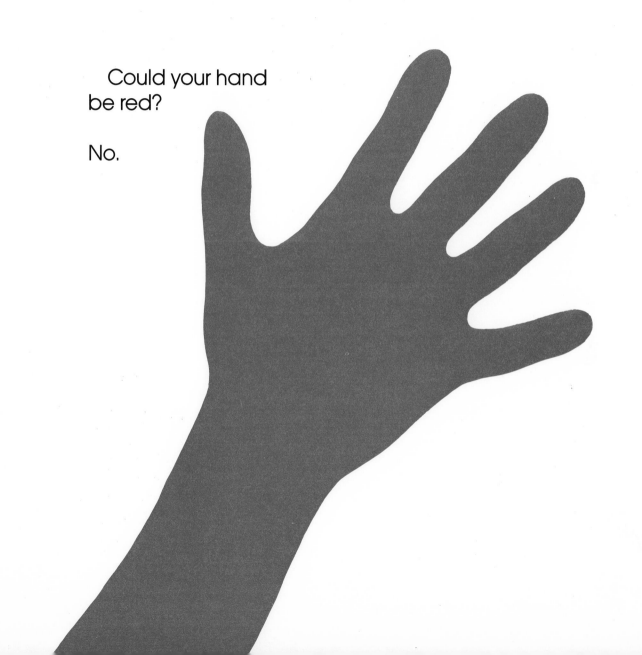

Sometimes
we say there are red people.
But there aren't really red people.
God saved pure red for apples

and tulips

and roses.

A truly red person

or a truly yellow person

would be very strange indeed!

We say some people are black,
but God didn't really make
people black.

Put your hand on this page.
This page is black.
Is your hand black?

No.

You may be brown,
or dark brown, or tan,
or a little pink,
or even a bit orange,
but not truly black.

God saved pure black
for deep, deep under the sea
and for parts of outer space
that, so far,
only a few lucky people
have seen.

In fact, God used
very little true black
in the world,
except perhaps for obsidian,
which is a beautiful black rock
that He lets volcanoes make
for Him
      (according to His
           plan).

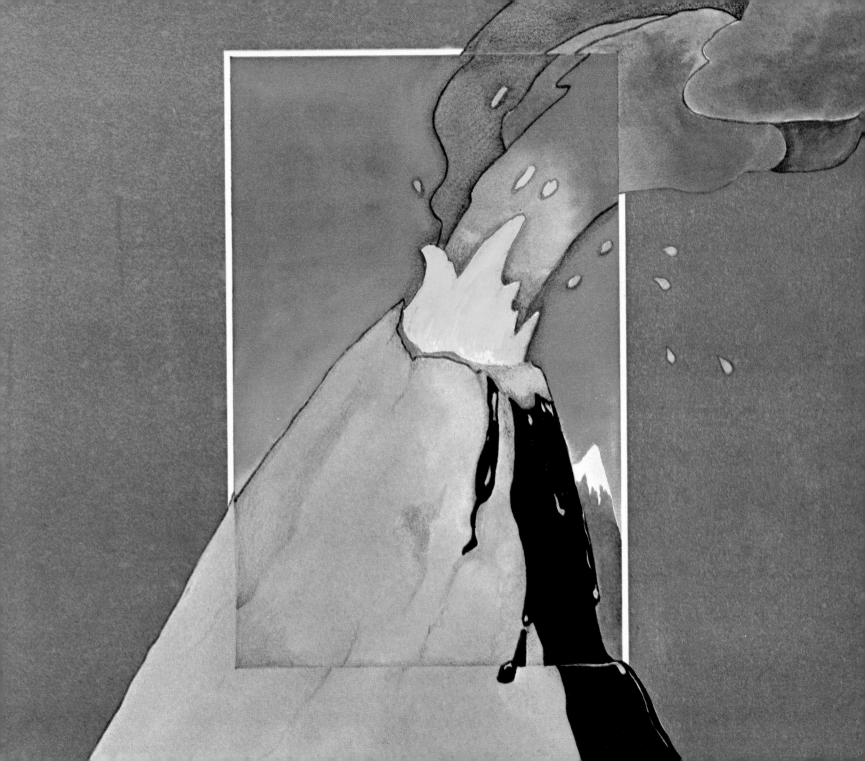

Even the night
is a dark, dark blue

and not
really black.

Sometimes
clowns color their faces
truly white or truly black
with truly red noses
and truly yellow hair.

But God didn't.

What color am I?
Not red.
Not black.
Not yellow.
Not white.
I may be brown, or dark brown,
or tan, or a little pink, or even a bit orange,
because these are the colors God planned
for
His
people.